RAISING RILEY

Published by Ducks Unlimited, Inc.
D. A. (Don) Young, Executive Vice President, Publisher
Book design by Michael Todd

ISBN: 1-932052-20-8

Published September, 2004

Ducks Unlimited, Inc.
Ducks Unlimited conserves, restores, and manages wetlands and associated habitats for North America's waterfowl. These habitats also benefit other wildlife and people. Since its founding in 1937, DU has raised more than $2 billion, which has contributed to the conservation of over 11 million acres of prime wildlife habitat in all fifty states, each of the Canadian provinces, and in key areas of Mexico. In the U.S. alone, DU has helped to conserve over 2 million acres of waterfowl habitat. Some 900 species of wildlife live and flourish on DU projects, including many threatened and endangered species.

Call to Action
The success of Ducks Unlimited hinges upon each member's personal involvement in the conservation of North America's wetlands and waterfowl. You can help Ducks Unlimited meet its conservation goals by volunteering your time, energy, and resources; by participating in our conservation programs; and by encouraging others to do the same. To learn more about how you can make a difference for the ducks, call 1-800-45-DUCKS.

Distributed by:
The Globe Pequot Press
P.O. Box 480
Guilford, CT 06437-0480

RAISING RILEY

Doug Truax

Illustrated by Jack K. Smith

DUCKS UNLIMITED

Ducks Unlimited, Inc.
Memphis, Tennessee

The pitch was right over the middle. Tyler swung the bat as hard as he could.

WHACK.

The ball sailed over the garage roof.

Man, I really smacked that one, Tyler thought, proudly.

CRASH.

"What's he done NOW!" Tyler's father screamed, looking at what remained of the front window of their house. Glass was scattered all over the living room. "Tyler!"

Tyler's mother looked on with a bit more patience.
"Yelling won't help," she said.

That evening Tyler and his mom and dad were relaxing in the family room.

"Listen to this," Mom said, reading from the newspaper. "For Sale: Yellow Lab retriever pups. Good breeding. Need good homes."

Hmmm, Tyler's dad thought. *Maybe that's what Tyler needs to channel his energy. A puppy. A pet he could learn to take care of and help train. And a dog they could hunt ducks with one day.*

Eight little yellow Lab puppies scampered around the kennel owned by the dog breeder who had advertised puppies for sale.

"How do we know which one to pick?" Tyler asked.

"They all look cute, don't they," his dad said.

They played with all the puppies. Turned them on their backs and gave them a soft belly rub. Played tug-of-war with a rag bone. But the longer Tyler and his parents stayed in the kennel, the more one little puppy kept following Tyler. Whenever Tyler knelt down, the puppy got on its hind legs and gave him a big lick on the face.

"I like this one," Tyler said.

"I think the feeling is mutual," Dad added.

"**G**ive it HERE, boy!" Tyler yelled. "That's my favorite sneaker. HERE. GIVE IT HERE!"

Mom looked on. "I think puppy needs a name. Otherwise we'll never get him to come to us."

"How about Jaws," Tyler's dad said. "There's nothing he won't chew."

They made a list of their favorite names and read them all again. None of them seemed right. Finally Tyler said, "How about Riley? Dad always says I live the life of Riley. Nothing to do but play and eat."

Mom and Dad nodded in agreement. Riley was just right.

Riley had a kennel in the kitchen where they could put him at night and close the door. Dad always got up first in the morning. He would open the kennel door and let Riley out in the fenced back yard to do his "business."

Tyler's job was to feed Riley twice a day. After Riley ate, Tyler took him out into the yard. Tyler also made sure the water bowl was always full.

"**D**AD," Tyler screamed, "RILEY POOPED IN THE KITCHEN!"

Sure enough, there was the evidence right in the middle of the floor. Riley trotted up to Tyler, wagging his tail like nothing in the world was wrong.

"BAD DOG," Tyler yelled, "BAD DOG."

"**Y**elling at him won't help," Dad said. "He doesn't speak your language and he has no idea what he did wrong."

Dad explained that the way they would train Riley would be to make obedience seem like play and to give him rewards for doing things right.

"We'll start that training tomorrow at feeding time," Dad said. "Right now you and I have to clean up this mess. That's one of the joys of being a dog owner," he said, laughing.

Yuk, Tyler thought, *I think I'm going to throw up*.

The next night Dad showed Tyler the first lesson—to sit. He put the food in the bowl, like Tyler always did. Then he raised it over Riley's head just a bit. Riley looked up at the food and, as he did, he sat down on his hind legs so he could see the food better. Dad then lowered the bowl to the ground and said "Good boy." Riley pounced on the food like he was starving.

Dad told Tyler to do the same thing for the next few nights.

Some nights Riley would jump and run around in little circles when Tyler raised the bowl. But Tyler would not lower it until Riley looked up at the food and sat down. Sometimes Tyler helped him sit with a gentle push on his back end. Then Tyler would say "Good boy" and lower the food.

Dad explained that the best way to train a dog was to help him do what came naturally.

One day before the evening feeding, Dad said, "Now, we'll teach him a word or two."

He told Tyler to raise the bowl like he had been doing but this time say the word "Sit" in a firm voice.

Tyler tried it. He filled the bowl and when Riley sat, Tyler said "Sit."

"Just right," Dad said. "You waited until he was doing the right thing, and then gave the command. Pretty soon he'll know that the word 'sit' means to put his rear end on the ground and not move."

It wasn't long before Riley would sit every time Tyler said "Sit" even if he wasn't being given his bowl of food. In the yard, Tyler would say "Sit" and then walk away and Riley would not budge. Sometimes Tyler would give him a small dog biscuit as a treat.

The next lesson was to teach Riley to heel. That meant that Riley would walk right beside Tyler with his nose near Tyler's knee. Tyler used a leash to walk Riley around the yard. When the puppy was close to his knee he would say "Heel," and then tell him what a good boy he was. It wasn't long before Riley really liked walking next to Tyler.

When the puppy was a few weeks older, Dad said Riley was ready to begin more serious schooling.

"Let's take him to the park and begin retrieving lessons," Dad said.

Dad brought a long leash and a couple of dummies. The dummies looked like small canvas pillows with a rope on one end.

They found a part of the park where no one was and Dad took Riley off the leash. Tyler grabbed the rope on the end of the dummy, swung it in a circle in the air, and let it fly. Riley watched it sail through the air and land way out in the field. He chased after it, grabbed it in his mouth, and brought it back.

"**H**e sure loves doing this," Tyler said, "just like he loves bringing our shoes and slippers."

"Dogs do some things because they are born to do them," Dad said. "It's called instinct. Retrievers are born with the love of bringing things back in their mouth."

"But now we come to the hard part," Dad explained. "We need to teach him to wait when we throw the dummy. Dogs, just like people, need to do some things that *don't* come naturally."

Tyler took the leash off Riley the next time they went to the field and said "Sit." Riley sat. But just as Tyler was about to throw the dummy, Riley spotted some squirrels playing in the field and chased after them.

"NO! RILEY GET BACK HERE. YOU SIT RIGHT NOW," Tyler shouted.

"Remember, there's no need to yell," Dad said, after they rounded up Riley. Dogs are related to wolves, he explained. Wolves live in packs and the leader of the pack is in charge of all the other wolves.

"Now you're the leader of Riley's pack," Dad said. "Take charge like the pack leader does. Look him right in the eyes and stand tall. Let him know you are the boss without making a lot of noise. That's how the wolves do it."

Tyler threw the dummy several more times and said "Sit" each time. Every bone in Riley's body wanted to race after it, but Riley sat still until Tyler said, "Go Fetch."

When they were done with the lesson in the field, Dad took Tyler to the ice cream shop. Riley waited in the car.

"You're becoming a very good trainer," Dad said. "You deserve a treat, too."

"Just like Riley, right?" Tyler said. "Only my treat sure beats a dog biscuit."

Tyler ordered a scoop of strawberry, his favorite flavor. As he sat on the bench eating his cone, Tyler felt proud to be called Riley's trainer.

Tyler and Dad kept training Riley every evening before dinner. They would usually spend 15 minutes and then just play and have fun until it was time to eat.

Their favorite place to play was a little lake in the park. Riley loved the water, and Tyler liked throwing sticks that Riley would swim after and bring back to shore in his mouth.

Riley became so well behaved, they could walk him in town when they went shopping or take him to the farmer's market on Saturday. Riley enjoyed meeting people and other dogs.

Every time they crossed a street Tyler would tell the young dog to "Heel" and they would walk safely across.

Riley followed Tyler everywhere.

One day, without giving it a thought, Tyler picked up his bat and ball, threw the ball in the air, and took a strong swing at it. This time he was careful to hit it away from the house. No more broken windows for him.

WHACK. Tyler hit the ball cleanly and it sailed across the yard and arched over the street.

Out of the corner of his eye, Tyler saw Riley bounding after the ball as it flew through the air. At the same instant, he caught a glimpse of another object moving that way. Terrified, he realized it was a car speeding down the street. The car and Riley were on a collision course!

"SIT," Tyler screamed at the top of his lungs. Riley was going full-speed, but he made a sudden stop and sat just short of the road as the car raced by. The ball rolled harmlessly into the neighbor's yard.

Tyler ran to Riley, fell on his knees, and gave him a big hug. "Gooood boy," he said. "Riley, you're the best dog in the world."